emotionary

Say what you feel

PALABRAS
ALADAS

PALABRAS ALADAS

Copy-editing and proof-reading: Jane Hammett

First published in 2016 by
Palabras Aladas, S. L.
Ronda de Valencia, 8
28012 Madrid
www.palabrasaladas.com

ISBN: 978-84-941513-6-1
Legal deposit: M-38662-2015
Printed by Sagrafic in Spain

SUGGESTION FOR READING

The chapters are written in the order of a real emotional journey. However, you can start with any emotion you like and go directly to its page.

TABLE OF CONTENTS

emotionary

Text: Cristina Núñez Pereira and Rafael R. Valcárcel

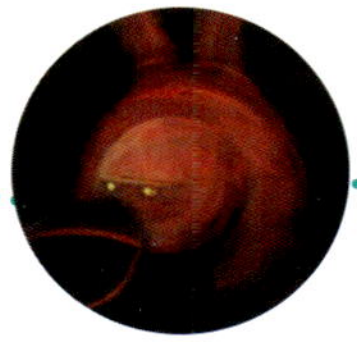

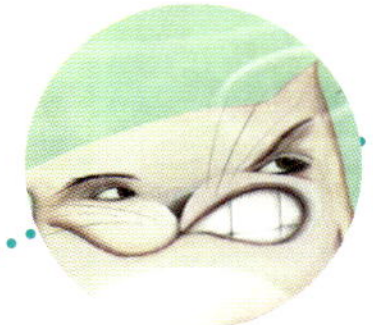

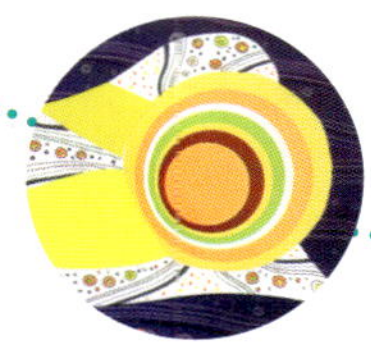

PROLOGUE

Rosa Collado Carrascosa

An EMOTIONARY. What a fantastic idea to help a person get to know themselves.

This EMOTIONARY will help even the youngest reader to recognise their emotions and discuss their feelings. This makes it possible to channel those emotions properly, in turn allowing us to reach our full potential, without compromising our abilities.

The EMOTIONARY can be seen as a fundamental pedagogical support. It allows the development of a child's emotional intelligence, which is key to his or her self-acceptance and to healthy psycho-evaluative development. For us to be happy, we must learn to integrate an understanding of our emotions into our psychological development.

The discovery, identification and differentiation of our emotions through this EMOTIONARY provides young readers with a safe educational context in which to discover themselves and to grow into emotionally self-aware adults with the sensitivity required to meet life's challenges.

Experiencing emotion is a human privilege, and learning to express our emotions will help us get closer to those we love.

Emotions are instinctive or intuitive states that affect our bodies, minds and how we behave. The purpose of emotions is to help us to deal with what is happening around us.

Feelings provide you with information about yourself and how you are reacting to a particular emotional state. Feelings serve as a way of expressing/communicating our emotions – to ourselves and also to others.

Rosa Collado Carrascosa is an experienced psychologist and psychotherapist.

Information for grown-ups.

Tenderness

Some living things stir our tenderness: a puppy, a sprouting tree, a new-born baby... Tenderness is closeness, affection and compassion.

We feel tender towards people, creatures and things that are defenceless or non-threatening.

Where is tenderness?

Tenderness is inside all of us. But it takes others to open the door to our tenderness. Their fragility awakens our desire to be kind, attentive and understanding.

Tenderness is an invitation to **love**.

Love

Of all the emotions, love is perhaps the most contradictory. It can be responsible for gigantic smiles or fountains of tears.

What types of love are there?

There is romantic love – when you are always thinking about a person and when seeing them produces a mix of excitement and joy. Then there's the kind of love where you share the happiness and the sadness someone else feels as if it were your own, and you always want the best for them. Love is a pure, warm feeling.

Love is the opposite of **hate**.

Hate

Hate is a great dislike – a feeling of repulsion – for something or someone. As a consequence, we wish bad things to happen to the object of our hate.

How long does hate last?

Sometimes hate lasts for a long time. Sometimes it just lasts a short while. You can feel a momentary hate for someone, but it doesn't mean you have stopped loving them.

If we act on our hate, we risk succumbing to **anger**.

Anger

Also known as rage, ire or fury. Anger is fleeting. It can rise up inside and take control of you then recede, almost without you even noticing. You're most likely to feel angry in situations that you consider very unfair, or when your wellbeing is under threat.

Is anger useful?

In a civilised society, no, because anger clouds your ability to think. It makes you react like an animal that is being attacked.

Since we don't live among wild beasts, such reactions tend to get us into trouble. That's why it's best to try to avoid letting anger take control before it's too late, such as when we begin to feel a little **irritated**.

Irritation

The world is full of colours, smells and sounds... Some, we like. Others, we may not like. Some even irritate us: they bother us so much that they get inside our heads and we can't stop thinking about them.

A puppy can arouse your tenderness. But what if it doesn't stop barking all day?

What happens when you are irritated?

When something irritates you, you become very aware of it. Something annoying becomes irritating when you believe you cannot stand it any more.

An irritation that lasts a long time can lead to **stress**.

Stress

Some people call it tension. We suffer stress when we face situations we consider threatening, such as:

—Moving house, or starting a new school

—Being in the middle of a heated discussion or argument

—Having a surprise test at school, when you haven't studied the topic.

You might also feel stressed when what you want to do doesn't fit in with what others want: for example, if you want to sleep but your neighbour wants to practise playing his new drums.

What happens when you feel stressed?

You are nervous and impatient and you lose your cool easily.

Speaking to someone you trust about what is causing your tension will help, and you will feel a great sense of **relief**.

Relief

We experience relief when we take a load off our mind, when we stop feeling threatened by something, or when we say sorry. For example, you'll feel relieved finishing an exam, when you see that a danger has passed, or even when you admit that you have been wrong and apologise. Relief means that an unpleasant feeling or situation has come to an end.

How do we get relief?

It usually comes when we relax.

Once we are relieved of our difficulties, our peace returns. We feel calm. This is the road to **serenity**.

Serenity

Serenity is a sensation of calm and harmony. It is born deep inside you, but it shows up most in your eyes. A serene person is tranquil, peaceful and always asks nicely when they want something.

Does serenity illuminate the mind?

Yes. It does so by giving you a special way of seeing things. It's like a superpower, with which you can see more clearly what is happening and what has happened. Thanks to your serenity, you can avoid getting angry when you realise that something isn't really worth getting angry about.

Curiously, you can exercise serenity as if it were a muscle. Training it will help you increase your **happiness**.

Happiness

Happiness feels different for each and every one of us. We are happy when we use our skills or talents – things we do well or enjoy doing.

What can make you happy?

Planting an orange tree, completing a puzzle, baking a cake, hanging a picture, writing a poem, solving a maths problem... there are lots of activities that can make you happy if you see them as an opportunity to enjoy yourself.

Happiness is a feeling of satisfaction with yourself. It is not to be confused with **delight**.

Salida

Delight

Some people call delight joy or glee.

Delight is caused by something pleasant and, for that reason, it's extremely enjoyable. In contrast to happiness or contentment, which can last a long time, delight is more intense and more short-lived. However, you can have lots of delightful moments throughout the day.

What happens in those moments?

A playful pleasure comes over you. You feel more energetic and you think more positively.

In moments of delight, we easily forget our **sadness**.

Sadness

Sadness is a general decline in our energy and our mood. When we are sad, we may lose our appetite, our strength, our drive... basically, our love of life.

Sadness is like a grey veil that can shroud our life.

What causes sadness?

Not everybody feels sad about the same things. Nevertheless, it's normal to feel sad when people let us down or we lose something important to us. Imagine you had to move to another city. You might feel excited about the new friends you would make and the new experiences you would have, but you would feel sad when you thought of all the friends you had left behind.

Sadness is part of **compassion**.

Compassion

Some people call it sympathy. We feel compassion (or pity) for others' misfortune.

What does compassion motivate us to do?

It motivates us to help those who are suffering, whether they are family members or complete strangers. They could even be characters that exist only inside a book, such as a fox that has lost his family. Our compassion makes us want to hug him to relieve his sadness.

If someone is feeling sad and we don't help them, we might enter the territory known as **remorse**.

Remorse

Some people confuse remorse with regret.

Regret is the uncomfortable feeling we might have after doing something we wished we hadn't or not doing something we wished we had. Remorse, however, only appears when we do something we know was wrong.

For example, you might regret having said "no" when your sister offered you some of her chocolate... but you'd certainly feel remorseful if you took some of her chocolate without asking.

How does remorse work?

It is simple but effective. Remorse doesn't allow you to think about anything else apart from the bad thing you did. It starts with mild discomfort, but little by little it grows inside you.

That discomfort that gnaws away at you is called **guilt**.

Guilt

Guilt creeps in when we believe we have done something wrong. It's part of our moral compass: it helps us understand what we consider to be good and what we consider to be bad. It also allows us to think about – and evaluate – our behaviour.

Can you hear guilt?

When you do something you know isn't right, a voice inside speaks to you. Listen to it. It is your conscience asking you to consider if you have behaved well – or not. Deep down, you know what's right and wrong, even if you sometimes choose not to listen to that voice.

Guilt reminds us that we are responsible for our own actions and enables us to judge them. If we realise we have made a mistake or behaved badly, we might feel **embarrassed**.

Embarrassment

Embarrassment appears unexpectedly. You feel it when you know you have made a mistake or when you think people are going to laugh at you.

Although it seems unlikely, it's possible to feel embarrassment for something that another person has done.

Can you hide embarrassment?

No. Embarrassment, unfortunately, is not very discreet. It exists to let others know that you are aware of your error. It makes your face turn red.

The fact that everybody else knows you are embarrassed can even cause **insecurity**.

Insecurity

Insecurity is a lack of confidence. We can lack confidence in ourselves, as well as in others.

Imagine yourself in a sailing boat at sea on a rough day. If you don't think you're a strong swimmer, you'll feel insecure, especially if you don't trust the boat's captain.

What happens when you feel insecure?

When you feel insecure, you adopt defence mechanisms. If you're not sure about your ability to swim, you'll panic (even though that's not a very useful reaction).

If you lose trust in a friend, you may want to isolate yourself from that friend to feel safer.

Sometimes, when we feel insecure, we can become **shy**.

Shyness

Shyness stops us from behaving naturally. It tends to get the better of us around strangers or people who seem untrustworthy or threatening.

How does a shy person feel?

A shy person feels uncomfortable and clumsy. They fear saying or doing something wrong, so they stay still and quiet in order not to be noticed.

Imagine that you have to spend the night with some elderly neighbours. Even though they are kind to you, you stay silent at one end of the sofa. You don't feel at ease. You might even begin to feel **confused**.

Confusion

Confusion is a messy mix of feelings. Imagine your puppy has chewed up your favourite toy. You'd feel angry, but you might also feel tender.

We experience confusion when we are not sure what is expected of us, or what to do in a given situation. It paralyses us. Sometimes we could find ourselves simultaneously feeling admiration, sadness, and perhaps even jealousy.

How do you recognise confusion?

If you are confused, you won't know exactly what is happening to you. Relax, though. It happens to us all from time to time. Try to work out what emotions are contributing to your confusion.

Unexpected and sudden confusion can lead to **fear**.

Fear

Also known as fright.

Fear appears when you think you're going to get hurt.

If fear is allowed to grow too much, it turns into terror and makes you lose control. Fear can help you stay alert in the face of danger – but terror paralyses you and stops you from thinking clearly.

What happens when you feel fear?

Your pupils dilate to let in more light, so you can see better. Also, your heart pumps more blood to your legs so you can run away, as you would if you were being chased by a dragon.

The unknown can cause fear, but it can also cause **astonishment**.

Astonishment

We encounter astonishment when something we think is impossible turns out to be true.

Astonishment tells us that the world is full of new things to discover and that there is a place for the unknown, for the magical. It reminds us that we are surrounded by fascinating people and things.

Where does astonishment come from?

Astonishment comes from innocence and curiosity. When you are astonished, you first believe that something is not possible. Later, you see that it is, and you feel excited. Then you ask yourself, "How is this possible?"

When accompanied by repulsion, astonishment can turn into **disgust**.

Disgust

Disgust is the displeasure that something repulsive makes us feel.

If you ask your parents about when you were a baby, you'll find that you did things then that might disgust you now. You might have eaten a worm in the garden, for example. That's why it would be interesting to ask yourself if disgusting things really exist, or whether it's just that your tastes and perceptions have changed.

Is everyone disgusted by the same things?

Everyone feels disgust towards something – but that something is different from family to family and place to place, because we learn what should disgust us from those around us.

Imagine a family from another culture have invited you to dinner at their house. To welcome you, they offer you their favourite food: insect salad. Showing your disgust could arouse their **hostility**.

Hostility

We feel hostile when someone stops us from doing what we want to do. For example, you are desperate to go out and play in the park, but it's too late so your parents won't let you.

When we feel hostile, we tend to disagree with everything we hear. If someone says "white", we say "black". If someone says "I like pineapple", we say "I hate it."

Where does hostility lead us?

Hostility leads us to reject others. We want to make them uncomfortable, attack them or upset them in some way.

If, instead of being hostile towards someone, you let them into your life, you are showing **acceptance**.

Acceptance

We feel acceptance when we are loved for who we are – for our good points as well as for all the things that aren't so nice about ourselves.

We also feel acceptance when others recognise and value our skills and deeds.

Which gestures demonstrate acceptance?

Applause, warm words, a smile, a hug and any other gesture whose purpose is to show us that we are appreciated.

A lack of acceptance makes us feel **misunderstood**.

Being misunderstood

We experience this when others fail to understand us. We try to explain something that is happening or what we are thinking, but others don't get it.

Sometimes, we feel misunderstood because people don't like something we are doing. Don't worry! Think about Leonardo da Vinci and other such geniuses. Many had to face being misunderstood because their thinking challenged the thinking of their time.

How do people end up being misunderstood?

You feel misunderstood when the way you see the world is different from the way others think you ought to see it. It feels like a mix of frustration and **helplessness**.

Helplessness

Helplessness comes when you feel unprotected; when you can't count on anyone's support. You can also feel helpless when you are unable to defend yourself or to help someone else.

It's a sensation of sorrow and sadness.

It happens, for example, if your friends don't support you or if they abandon you.

What do you think when you feel helpless?

You think that if you ask for help, nobody will come to your aid.

You can be surrounded by people, but if you don't have their backing, you can experience **solitude**.

Solitude

Solitude is the absence of company. It can be quite useful – for example, if you don't want anyone to bother you. But it can also lead to loneliness if you don't have anyone to turn to or to share things with.

Is it possible to feel lonely when you're with other people?

Yes, when you can't count on the people around you or when they make you feel unwanted. Imagine that all your friends are talking about a film that you haven't seen. If you can't take part in the conversation, you might feel lonely.

To overcome unwanted solitude, it's important to communicate with those around you.

If you keep thinking about a happy time in your life when you were surrounded by friends, you're being **nostalgic**.

Nostalgia

Nostalgia creates an empty space in our hearts and, just as it appears, it fills up with drops of sorrow.

Nostalgia may strike when you are missing somebody you used to know, or something you did in the past. This feeling of absence quickly saddens us.

How do we identify nostalgia?

If remembering makes us sad, that's nostalgia.

When nostalgia begins to play a part in our everyday life, we become prisoners to **melancholy**.

Melancholy

Melancholy is an extreme form of nostalgia, a form of sadness. When we are melancholic, we feel that the world we want to live in is far away and difficult to reach.

When does melancholy appear?

Melancholy often strikes during periods of change. At such times, for example on Sunday afternoons, we might feel melancholic about the fact that our fun weekend is coming to an end.

The allure of melancholy may cause you to become absorbed in it, making you forget about the here and now. However, when it passes, you risk feeling overcome with **boredom**.

b a
c 1
2
d 3
4
e

Boredom

Also known as weariness or indifference.

Boredom is a mix of annoyance and tiredness that we feel when we don't have anything to do, or when what we are doing doesn't satisfy us.

It's like a worm that eats away at our ability to enjoy ourselves.

What's the relationship between boredom and time?

When we are bored, time seems to pass more slowly. It str-e-e-e-e-e-tches out.

A good antidote to boredom is to come up with some ideas that arouse our **excitement**.

Excitement

Excitement is the anticipation we feel when something we want is coming soon. Being excited is one of the best ways to enjoy life, and being excited gives us energy.

Are some things naturally exciting, or do we make them exciting?

We can get excited about practically anything: a new brother or sister being born, celebrating our birthday, going to school, playing with friends.... Excitement is one of life's most tasty ingredients.

Being excited sparks our **enthusiasm**.

Enthusiasm

Enthusiasm is the waking of an inner god. When we surrender to it, we feel almighty and capable of anything.

What does enthusiasm sound like?

Enthusiasm sounds like music because your heart beats to a special rhythm. Listen out for the song of enthusiasm inside your body. The rhythm starts off in your heart and, as it gathers pace, it runs along your arms and down your legs. It's an energy that is born inside you and spurs you into action.

Energised by this music, we can easily become **euphoric**.

Euphoria

Euphoria is an overflowing of positive energy. It gives you the strength to face moments of adversity or to celebrate with unusual enthusiasm.

What does euphoria feel like?

A feeling of extraordinary wellbeing and optimism, and of being capable of rising to any challenge.

Euphoria is the opposite of **discouragement**.

Discouragement

We feel discouraged when we lack the courage to carry on with something; when we notice how tired we are; and when we realise that what we are trying to achieve isn't so easy after all.

Imagine you are in a forest and you want to find your way home. You take a route that doesn't lead there. You trace your footsteps back to your starting point and try another route – but it's not that one either. You keep trying but, again, you fail to find the path home. On the fourth try, you lose faith that you are going to get home at all, and you feel like giving up. That is discouragement.

What happens when we become discouraged?

The nearer we are to discouragement, the further away our goals feel.

When discouragement beats us and we give in, we open the door to **disappointment**.

Disappointment

This is the negativity that invades you when you realise that a "truth" you were comfortable with is not true at all.

You can also feel disappointed when people – or things – fail to live up to your expectations.

Is it possible to never be disappointed?

That could only happen if you already knew everything – absolutely everything! – from how many times your mum will smile at you in the morning to the exact size of the universe. If you can be surprised, you can also be disappointed, because both emotions mean that something isn't as we thought, or expected. If you are disappointed, things are worse than you had imagined. But there's no need to feel down. These experiences also help us to learn.

As you see, it's practically impossible to never experience disappointment. Nevertheless, it is possible to avoid falling foul of **frustration**.

Frustration

This is the annoyance you feel when you don't achieve something you set out to achieve.

What usually leads to frustration?

—Our own limitations, such as not being old enough to take part in a competition.

—The limitations or decisions of others, such as when you can't go to a fun after-school activity because it's been cancelled.

—The weather: for example, a summer storm that prevents you from going to the beach.

Faced with the same situation, some people get frustrated – while others look for solutions. The latter can provoke our **admiration**.

2

Admiration

Admiration is the respect we feel for someone who has great qualities or who has done something extraordinary. For example:

—a sportsperson who constantly strives to better themselves

—an explorer who travels to an unknown jungle

—a friend who can draw really well.

Is there something to admire in everyone?

Yes, but sometimes you have to look hard to find it. Some people have qualities that we don't, or they are able to do things that we can't. For that reason, we admire them.

To admire others, we need to be aware of our own limitations. If doing so makes you unhappy and stops you from appreciating them, you have fallen into the trap of **envy**.

Envy

Some people say that envy and jealousy are the same. This, however, is not the case – although these emotions do go hand in hand and feed off each other. They suck the joy out of you. They don't care if you grow and improve. They are simply concerned that others around you don't.

What's the difference between jealousy and envy?

Jealousy makes it difficult for you to share what you consider to be yours, like the attention of a loved one. Envy, on the other hand, doesn't focus on what you have, but on what others have. You might feel envious when someone has something you **desire**.

Desire

Desire is an attraction towards something we want. We may desire things we don't have, which makes us set about trying to get them. Desire drives us to act.

You can desire a great many things, such as to grow up, to learn to swim, to spend time with your grandparents, or to become a fireman.

Are all desires the same?

No. Some desires are very strong and profound. For instance, you might desire to be a doctor, so you are motivated to study for a long time to qualify. Some desires are more like whims: they are more fleeting. For example, thinking about Christmas dinner might make you crave mince pies.

A fulfilled desire gives us **satisfaction**.

Satisfaction

Fulfilling a need brings satisfaction.

That need can be physical or emotional: a basic need such as hunger, for example, or an artistic need, such as to paint a landscape. When you eat, or finish your painting, you feel satisfaction.

Does satisfaction help to build your confidence?

Yes! It improves your self-confidence, especially when the satisfaction is as a result of something you have done well. You feel doubly satisfied, for example, when you eat some tomatoes that you helped to grow.

Satisfaction can even be experienced in defeat.

Losing a competition but feeling you have performed well can still be a great achievement. Constant improvement fills you with **pride**.

Pride

Pride is noticing the value in ourselves or someone or something we love.

The personal pride you feel for who you are or what you do can both benefit and hinder you.

What types of personal pride are there?

—Selfish pride, which tends to make being the centre of attention your number-one goal. As a consequence, you might become aloof or arrogant.

—Virtuous pride, which makes your number-one goal to constantly strive to be the best you can. It allows you to discover and value your qualities. As a consequence, it can help you to overcome great challenges.

Improving yourself brings **pleasure**.

Pleasure

Pleasure is the satisfaction and delight that is produced by something we really like.

You can find pleasure in all sorts of activities: fantasising about other worlds, looking at beautiful things, solving difficult problems, playing, feeling loved...

How can we appreciate pleasure?

To feel pleasure, you need to concentrate.

Imagine you have a glass of juice in front of you. You could drink it all quickly to quench your thirst. Or you could concentrate on the flavour and enjoy it slowly. With pleasure, you get out what you put in.

Living a life full of pleasure makes us **grateful**.

Gratefulness

Gratefulness, or gratitude, is the soul of the phrase "thank you". It is multiplied every time you see a gift in the ordinary and everyday: in the smile of a friend, in a song.

Gratefulness teaches you to appreciate life more. It paves the way to happiness.

When I was ten years old, my grandma gave me a Diary of Thanks. She said to me:

"I have one the same. Every night, I write in it all the things that have made me grateful that day. Then, when I sleep, the contents and characters of my diary find their way into my dreams and fill the rooms of my Happy Palace... and the happiness they bring stays with me all the next day."

What have we written today?

—Thanks to all those who have filled the pages of this book with their magic.

—Thanks to the person who bought it for you.

—Most of all, thanks to you for sharing in our emotionary.